W9-AEI-572

COMMONSENSE

Instrument Care

STRING LETTER PUBLISHING

COMMONSENSE

Instrument Care

BY JAMES N. MCKEAN

STRING LETTER PUBLISHING

String Letter Publishing

PO Box 767

San Anselmo, California 94979

(415) 485-6946

www.stringsmagazine.com

Editor: Mary VanClay

Designer: Barbara Gelfand

Publisher: David A. Lusterman

Marketing: Jennifer Fujimoto

Production: Judy Zimola

All rights reserved.

No part of this publication may be reproduced, stored in a retrieval system, or transmitted, in any form or by any means, without the permission of String Letter Publishing.

Copyright James N. McKean, 1996   ISBN 0-9626081-9-X

10 09 08 07 06 05 04 03 02

CONTENTS

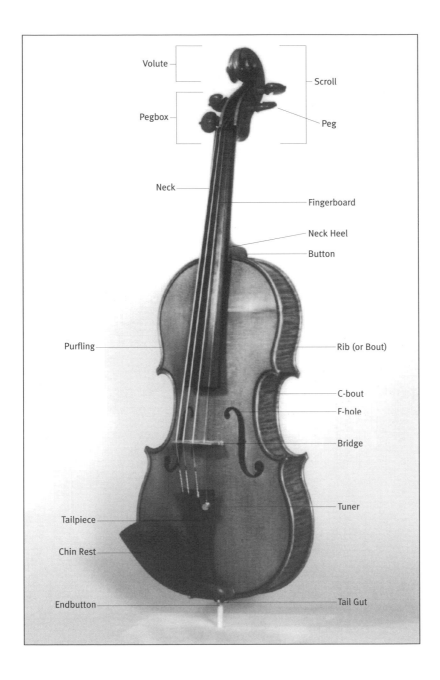

The various parts of the violin (and viola). They are the same for the cello, except for the chin rest, which the cello doesn't have; it has an endpin.

COMMONSENSE

Instrument Care

INTRODUCTION

Now that your long search is over and you have found your instrument, you might want to spend a few moments familiarizing yourself with it and learning how to take care of it. Just a small amount of preventive care on your part can save your investment. There are violins being played on today that were built four centuries ago; with the proper attention, you can assure that, when your instrument is handed on to the next generation, its condition will be as good as when you received it. Think of yourself as the custodian, rather than the owner. This guide will try to inform you about your violin—or viola or cello—and give you some tips on how to maintain it.

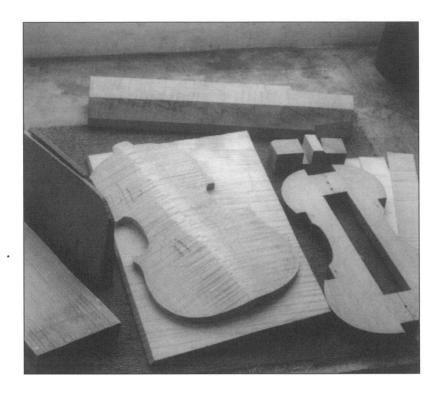

A joined back, with the rough outline cut; it is resting on a one-piece back. To the right is the form board that the violin will be built around. Beneath the form are the thin strips of maple that will be bent with steam to make the sides, or "ribs," and just above it are the small pieces of willow from which the corner and endblocks will be carved. At the top is the long piece of maple that will become the neck and scroll.

SOME BASICS

The choice of wood for an instrument is very important, for it is the first step in creating the character of the sound. The back, ribs, and neck of a violin are, almost without exception, made of maple. Violas and cellos, however, are often found with backs carved from poplar, a somewhat softer wood; it is used when the maker wants to produce a darker timbre to the sound. While poplar can have figure, it is usually plain. The maple that violin makers use, on the other hand, is marked with the distinctive tiger-striping referred to as "flame" or "curl." This figure is caused by a rippling of the grain as the tree grows; when the wood is scraped clean, the light hits the wood fibers at different angles, giving it the effect of alternating bands of light and dark.

The backs can be of one or two pieces; the latter is called "book-matched," for the billet of raw wood is split open like a book, and then joined down the middle. The way the wood is cut affects both its appearance and the way it will resonate. The sides of the instrument—also called the ribs, or bouts—are usually sawn from the same piece of wood as the back, and are formed by bending on a hot iron.

The arching of the back and top is carved out—first with a large gouge, and then with small brass thumb planes. The finishing is done with a steel scraper, to give the truest possible curves and a sheen to the wood that makes it glow under the varnish. After the arch is finished, the inside of the plate is then hollowed out. Just how thick to leave the wood is of critical importance for the sound of the completed instrument; these graduations are measured in tenths of a millimeter and must be adjusted for the tonal characteristics of each individual piece of wood.

The top is made from a wedge of spruce that has been split from the log to ensure the straightest possible grain. It is usually of two pieces, with narrower grain in the center for strength.

The pieces of the body are held together by the blocks and linings, made of either willow or spruce. They provide support and rigidity to the rib structure, anchor the neck and end-button, and reinforce the top and back. There are six blocks:

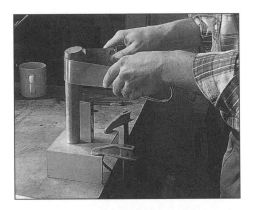

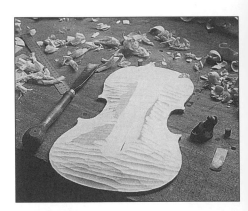

Making a violin. Clockwise, from upper left: When bending the ribs, the solid brass bending iron is hot enough to vaporize water. The arch of the top and back is roughed out with a gouge, and then finished with a thumb plane and scraper. The f-holes are cut with a knife. The inside is hollowed out, with the thicknesses graduated in tenths of a millimeter.

an upper and a lower, and one in each of the four corners. The linings, glued to the ribs, provide extra gluing surface for the top and back.

There are two other components found inside the instrument that play a vital role in its sound: the bass bar and the soundpost. Located under each foot of the bridge, they serve the dual role of supporting the top and distributing the sound when the instrument is played. A small part of the side of the bass bar can be seen through the left f-hole. Fitted and glued to the top, the bar runs almost the full length of the plate. The bass bar—how it is placed and shaped—provides one of the primary ways a violin maker can alter the sound and response of a finished instrument. The soundpost is a spruce dowel that is wedged (not glued) between the top and the back. A tool called the soundpost setter is used to insert the post through the f-hole, and then to move the post to adjust the balance and focus of the sound. The bridge, made of maple specially selected for its hardness, is fitted to the top and held in place by the pressure of the strings; as with the soundpost, the bridge's shape and placement can noticeably affect the sound of your instrument. (For further discussion of these components, see the chapters beginning on pages 31 and 37.)

The black and white strip around the edge of your instrument actually consists of three pieces of wood that are inlaid into the top and back. Called purfling, it is more than just decoration; it also serves as a binder to hold the edges together and help prevent cracks from developing. Some of the old Italian and English makers just scribed these lines on, rather than going through the time-consuming process of digging out the channel and hammering in the strips of wood. Contemporary makers usually use dyed pear wood for the black and poplar for the center, the same materials used by the classical Cremonese makers. A variety of other materials can be found—the Dutch makers frequently used whalebone for white and black, while the French often used ebony for black. Neopolitan makers such as the Gaglianos used paper—legend has it that it was the oiled paper used to wrap fish. Whatever is used, it is important that this binder be fit as well as possible—if an instrument develops a buzz, the first possibility to check is loose purfling rattling in its channel.

The neck and head of the violin are carved from a single piece of wood, usually maple. The neck is replaced when the

Purfling is made up of three strips of wood, inlaid into a groove that is cut around the edges of the top and back. While adding to the beauty of the instrument, its main purpose is as a binder, to help prevent cracks from developing when the weather changes.

old one wears out—a new piece of wood is grafted onto the old head, as it is very important for the value of the instrument that it retain its original scroll. The classical makers used nails to hold the head to the body of the instrument; modern makers fit and glue the neck into a dovetail joint. The angle at which the neck is set is very important for the sound of your instrument.

The fingerboard of the violin is made of ebony and, like the neck, must be replaced when it wears out. The fittings—the tailpiece, pegs, and chin rest—are also of a tropical hardwood, usually ebony or rosewood or, sometimes, boxwood.

Your instrument's bow is deceptively simple: a stick of wood and a frog to hold the hair. The bow reached its final form much later than the violin; it was not until the beginning of the 19th century, in Paris, that François Tourte perfected the design (his bows, like the instruments of Stradivari, are still considered to be without equal). The stick, for anything better than the cheapest grade of bow, is almost always made from a tropical hardwood called pernambuco, so called because it comes from the valley of the Pernambuco River in Brazil. It is an extremely dense wood—like ebony, it sinks in water—but it combines flexibility with great strength and durability. The bow maker graduates the stick in precise gradations (according to Tourte's system) so that it is evenly flexible throughout. The ideal bow allows the musician to draw a full stroke from frog to tip without feeling the slightest change in the way it grabs the string; it should also bounce quickly and evenly in spiccato passages.

The maker achieves the camber, or curve, of the bow by heating it over a flame and bending it. The shape and distribution of the camber are critical to your bow's performance, and altering them is an art. The weight of the bow falls within narrow parameters, with a variance of a few grams at most, and the balance point must also be precisely located for the bow to feel right. Contrary to what many people believe, the strength of the bow does not depend on its weight; French bows, which, in the antique market, are still considered the best, tend to be light. Much more important than weight are the balance and evenness of response. The selection of a bow is intensely personal—it has to match both you as a player and your instrument—and there is no question that the bow you use will affect the quality of sound you get from your instru-

The head is made up of the neck and scroll. They are originally carved from the same block of wood, which is usually
maple. When the neck wears out, a new one is grafted on so
that the instrument retains its original scroll.

ment. As with instruments, the perception still exists that older bows are better, but certainly there are bows being made today that, in materials, skill of workmanship, and pure artistry, rival any from the past.

The bow's frog is usually ebony, although traditionally, when bow makers have wanted to "dress up" a bow they consider better than average, they have used ivory or tortoiseshell. Since both these materials come from endangered species, their use and importation are now banned. Makers use substitutes for the frog, as as well as for the ivory tip and the black-and-white whalebone lapping that protects the lower end of the stick from wear from the forefinger. Mastodon tusk—often dug out of the Arctic ice—serves for ivory, while artificial resins have provided a reasonable substitute for tortoiseshell and whalebone. The lapping, as well as the tip, can also be of silver; the choice depends as much on weight and balance as personal preference. Between the lapping and the front of the frog is a wrapping called the grip, which is made of either leather or snakeskin.

The bow hair is knotted at each end and then inserted into cavities in the head and the frog, where it is held in place by fitted wooden plugs. A slide fits into the bottom of the frog; this is traditionally faced with abalone, sometimes of a wild pattern. As with the neck of the instrument, the slide frequently is not the original, and whether it is or not has no effect on the value. The other metal parts of the bow—the ferrule (the small semicircle covering the protruding tongue of the frog that holds the hair), the button, and the circles (if the bow has them) around the inlaid eyes on the sides of the frog—can be gold instead of silver, again marking a bow of extra merit. On more inexpensive bows, this metal is usually nickel.

The frog is held in place by a small screw that extends inside the end of the stick and is turned by the button. The screw goes through a threaded eyelet, which is attached to the frog; you can see it if you unscrew the button all the way (but be sure that the hair is not twisted before you screw it all back together).

When handling both both your instrument and your bow, a small amount of care will yield a lifetime of use. We'll take a closer look at what to do in the chapters ahead.

The inside of the instrument, in this case a rare viola made
by Matteo Goffriller in Venice in 1703. Visible are the corner
and endblocks and the linings, which are the narrow strips
glued to the ribs. The small square pieces of wood glued to
the back are called studs; they are reinforcements over
cracks. The lower right rib has had a doubling put over it, by
the corner block; this also reinforces a damaged area.

Inside the top. The long vertical piece of wood glued to the top by the right f-hole is the bass bar. More studs can be seen, in addition to the soundpost patch, which is by the left f-hole. The edge of the top has been doubled, no doubt due to the thinning of the original over time. This is new wood, extending about 1.5 cm in from the edge of the entire top.

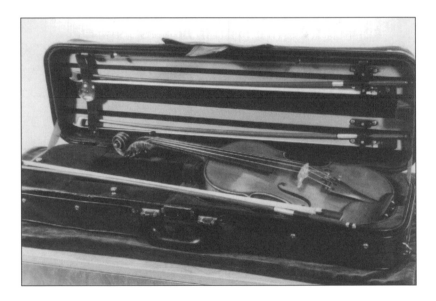

A suspension case (above). The instrument rests on padded steps so that the centers of the top and back do not come into direct contact with the case, better avoiding damage from impact. Resting your instrument on the case instead of in it (below) is not a good idea. The lid can easily fall, snapping the bow or sending the bridge through the top of the violin.

PREVENTING ACCIDENTS

Most of the repairs that find their way into a shop are the result of accidents that could easily have been prevented. The best way to avoid a costly repair is to exercise caution. Keep in mind that while your instrument was built to last for centuries, it is, after all, made of very thin wood that is subjected to a considerable amount of tension (the strings of a violin, when tuned up, exert roughly 40 pounds of pressure on the top—a piece of spruce that, at its thickest, barely reaches 3 mm). It's when you're not playing the instrument that accidents occur; as when caring for a small child, you only have to let your attention slip for a minute for trouble to happen.

Cellos are particularly vulnerable, due to their size. It's rare to find an old cello without its share of rib cracks or more serious damage. It's easy to see why—at any rehearsal break, for example, you'll see the cellos left propped on their sides on the stage, usually with a bow balanced on the ribs. You would be surprised at how easy it is to overlook a cello in spite of its size; when it's on the floor, surrounded by chairs and music stands, it's out of the line of sight.

Since you probably spend more time with your instrument and bow than you do with your family, you can very quickly forget how valuable and delicate they are. When you're not playing, put them away—the case isn't just for carrying them around. Put the instrument (and bow) in properly and close the case; an open lid can easily fall, causing serious damage. Also be sure to secure at least one of the latches. If you don't, you might forget the case is open and pick it up, sending the instrument tumbling to the ground. When cellists do put their instruments away, most of them leave the cases standing upright with the lid ajar, relying on a piece of Velcro (usually pretty worn) to restrain the cello—which shows a touching but misplaced faith in one of the products of modern technology.

If you leave the front of the case unfastened and the cello does fall out, it will land on the bridge. This directs the force of the impact directly onto the most critical part of the instrument, the area between the f-holes and the center of the back, where the soundpost sits. Repairing this damage requires major surgery; it also inevitably results in a change (usually for the worse) in the sound and response of your instrument, as well as a significant loss in its value. Leaving a cello case standing up, even when latched, is not a good idea anyway. Since a case's weight is a primary concern, they all taper at the lower end; but this makes them unstable when left standing on their own. If you do leave your case like this, make sure it is in a spot where it won't get bumped, and where there is something else (the piano, for example, or a dresser) to stop it from falling flat on the floor. If you don't want to put the cello away every time you stop playing, a company called Kempton's Standby Music Products (8135a Belvedere Ave., Sacramento, CA 95826; [916] 452-4909) makes a nifty cradle that will hold (and display) the instrument safely.

If you really want to protect your instrument, get a case with a suspension system. Designed to hold the instrument at its sturdiest points, the endblocks, these cases keep the weakest areas away from any contact with the case itself. As a result, the instrument isn't resting on its back; a standard case with no suspension system transmits any impact directly to the soundpost area. Many instruments, particularly cellos, also suffer damage from moving around inside most cases, but a suspension case holds the instrument securely when properly latched. If, when you open your case, you see a white line on the inside of the lid where the bridge touches it, then the case is not doing its job. The instrument is moving so that the bridge bumps against the inside of the top, and any impact will be transmitted directly to the instrument. You should be able to pick up your case when the instrument and bows are in it and shake it vigorously without hearing anything bumping around inside (try just a gentle shake first to make sure everything is secure). Most case manufacturers offer a line of suspension cases for violin and viola; less easy to find, but worth looking for, are those for cello. The Weber Case Co. makes an excellent cello suspension case, which can be found at most violin shops.

Cellists who travel any distance are forced to confront the unpleasant problem of what to do with the instrument on an airplane. The safest choice, of course, is to buy a seat, but that is frequently not an option; aside from the expense, there are airlines that won't allow cellos in the passenger cabin. Other carriers let you bring your cello on board but restrict you to the bulkhead seats—which are often unavailable, particularly at reduced fares. Checking the instrument as baggage can be very risky; you can be fairly certain that sooner or later it will result in some bad news. Many cellists try to lessen the risk by using travel cases, the heavy, metal-reinforced plastic containers you see cellists wheeling about in airports. You should be aware that while these cases might mitigate damage, they will not guarantee against it. In fact, they could even make things worse. The reason is simple: think of an automobile, whose primary design purpose—to get the occupant from one point to another as safely as possible—is the same as that of your instrument case. Cars are designed to absorb impact, so the exterior is meant to crumple up to help absorb the force of the collision before it reaches the occupant. Travel cases, though, are rigid. They are made of impact-resistant materials and reinforced to the point that they could probably withstand a nuclear attack. This means that the force of any impact is conducted directly to whatever is inside—your instrument. Travel cases are also very heavy, so when they fall, they land harder than a regular case does. A better solution is to find a soft, impact-absorbent bag that fits snugly around the cello case. Unfortunately, there aren't many of these on the market. The only one I have found that works is made by BAM, a French company; most violin shops will be glad to order one for you (the company's American distribution branch is BAM France, at 300 N. Elizabeth St., Suite 6S, Chicago, IL 60607; phone [312] 243-6691 or [800] 757-4226, or fax [312] 243-6693). If you are transporting your instrument and want to minimize the chance of anything happening to it, then a soft bag that fits well around a suspension case is your best bet. But just remember that you are still taking a chance.

Another course of action worth looking into is gate-checking, which allows you to check your instrument at the gate instead of the baggage counter. An attendant carries it to the plane and ensures that it is securely stowed in the luggage compartment; it is returned to you as you leave the plane. Not all airlines offer the service, and those that do won't necessarily make it available on every flight, so be sure to call ahead and verify that gate-checking is an option. Then have the airline issue you a separate ticket for the cello case. (It's actually a baggage-check slip, but it is usually printed out on the ticket form, because you have to pay extra for it. The additional cost is nominal, especially when compared to buying a seat.) My

A cello cradle displays your instrument nicely as well as holding it securely.

experience has been that airline personnel rarely know the procedures of their own company when it comes to this service, so insist on this piece of paper—you don't want to be faced with a different story and the need for long explanations at every step of the way. It's remarkable how a printed receipt clears the air.

Whatever you decide to do about the cello, there is one thing you shouldn't try: showing up at the gate at the last minute and talking your way on, cello in hand. It won't happen. You will still have several choices open to you, but they'll include missing the flight, buying a one-way ticket at the last minute for the cello, or checking it into baggage—not exactly what you had in mind.

A recent cello congress provided an excellent opportunity to test and compare the various ways of transporting the instrument. The most frequent choice was the heavy, reinforced flight case, checked into baggage. This method seemed to work pretty well, but one of my colleagues discovered how far from foolproof it really is: he opened the case upon arrival only to find the neck broken off his brand-new cello. It could have been worse; a neck graft is a major job, but at least it doesn't devalue the instrument, as a major crack in the back or top would. I took two instruments and had a change of planes, which afforded me several opportunities to see how different methods actually worked. I took the strings off both the cellos, to reduce tension on the instruments. One instrument I packed securely into a sturdy hard case, which I then put into a flight bag and checked into baggage. It arrived with a cracked top. The other I put in a suspension case, and I gate-checked it. That one arrived safely—but it almost didn't. I made the mistake of checking it in at the gate early, and after receiving the usual assurances about how well it would be cared for, I had the distinctly unsettling experience of watching the case as it was left standing on the tarmac next to the baggage ramp. It was a windy day, and the case went over, landed right on its front, and then bounced. I was lucky, because the cello was unscathed. But I learned a lesson: use gate-checking, but check the instrument at the very last minute. And don't be afraid to make a stink—stress how fragile it is, how valuable, and how well-insured. If the instrument really is irreplaceable, as most antique cellos are, then you should not even contemplate checking it.

You should also avoid putting your case in the trunk of your car. In the summer, the trunk can get very hot, very fast—hot enough to melt the varnish, crack the top, or loosen the glue that holds the instrument together. Using the trunk is a bad idea in any case; I've heard about several instruments reduced to splinters in a rear-end accident.

As for heat damage, the backseat can be just as bad as the trunk if the direct rays of the sun are on the case for any length of time. Most cases are covered in a dark material that will absorb the heat. If there is a chance that the sun might be on the case, cover it with a light-colored towel.

Instruments can suffer greatly from the extremes of weather, be it dryness in the winter or humidity in the summer. The former can cause cracks to develop as the wood shrinks, particularly on the top; it can also cause old repairs to open. Humidity, usually accompanied by heat, can soften the glue and the wood itself, causing the neck to drop, the sides to open, and old repairs to give way under the constant tension exerted on the instrument. These conditions create real problems that have few solutions; unless you are prepared to keep your instrument in museum conditions, you can't possibly eliminate the dangers caused by weather. You can, however, mitigate its effects.

Maintaining humidity in the winter is almost impossible; all you can really hope to do is temper the extremes of dryness. You can use a humidifier in the room where you keep your instrument, and you should keep the case away from radiators and heating vents. Of course, when you leave the humidified room and go out into the wider world, the instrument will be subjected to the greater dryness—and it is the sudden drop in humidity, as much as the dryness itself, that causes problems. You can, however, take some humidity along with you. Cases are designed to keep water out, and they work just as well to keep it in. You can use a commercial product like a Dampit, which is merely a long sponge enclosed in a protective tube, suspended in the body of the instrument through the f-hole. Dampits are sold in most shops; many musicians use two. You can also make a humidifier that operates on much the same principle by using an ice pick or small drill to liberally perforate a plastic soap holder. Put a damp sponge inside, and you have a humidification system you can keep in the case. Just be sure it isn't actually touching the instrument, and that it is placed so that it isn't rattling around (this device usually only fits in an oblong case). And remember, Dampits and sponges only work if they are damp. They will dry out quickly, so you'll have to rewet them at least once a day (more frequently in the depths of winter). It's a chore, but if using them properly will help stave off a visit to the repair department, then it is well worth it.

Adding humidity, as difficult as it is, is still nothing compared to trying to take it out. Summer weather presents real problems in most parts of the country, particularly as many instruments are used outdoors at festivals. Air-conditioning will reduce the level of humidity considerably, and you can also invest in a dehumidifier (you'll be surprised at how much water these appliances can take out of the air). You can also have an arch protector made for your instrument, if it is a violin or viola; this is no more than a wedge of cardboard that fits between the underside of the fingerboard and the top of the instrument. It takes some of the strain off the neck when you aren't playing it. Unfortunately, it won't work with the cello, the instrument that needs it most. Cellists have to resign themselves to a certain amount of neck movement between the seasons; most players have several bridges that they rotate as the neck goes up or down with the weather. It is only to be expected, as long as the range isn't too drastic; but if the seasonal difference is more than 5 mm, it could indicate structural problems in the neck, the upper block, or the top.

Considering how responsive instruments are designed to be, and how delicate they are compared to the amount of tension they are constantly subjected to, most of them are remarkably stable and durable. A modicum of care is all it takes, usually, to prevent a visit to the repair shop.

INSURANCE

Insurance is a must for any instrument that is worth more than the cost of the premium (which for most violins is relatively insignificant). Theft occurs all too frequently (but remember that few if any insurance policies will cover theft from your car). There are very few repairs that will cost less than the deductible, and if an instrument suffers an accident, the bill could easily run into the thousands of dollars. If you feel that your instrument is not of a value to warrant a separate policy, then be sure to put it on your homeowner's or householder's, if possible. You should get a written appraisal of the instrument when you purchase it, along with a detailed description done by a violin maker or repairer (who know which details are important to look for). Take a few moments and photograph the instrument from the front, back, and at an angle; these will help immeasurably in identifying it if it is ever stolen. The pictures don't have to be of professional quality; anything will help.

Whether you are an amateur or a professional, you should keep in mind the possibility of theft. Security backstage, particularly during rehearsals, is usually a joke. A violinist once told me that he left his Guarneri del Gesù in its case in a dressing room while he stepped down to the green room for a smoke; he returned only minutes later to find the case gone, along with the violin and his bows. He was lucky; everything turned up at a pawn shop within days. The famous violinist Bronislaw Huberman was not so fortunate; his Stradivari was stolen from its case backstage at Carnegie Hall while he was performing on his Guarneri del Gesù. The violin did reappear—but not until 50 years later, long after Huberman was dead. The fact is that stolen merchandise is seldom recovered. Instruments and bows might be unique, but it takes a trained eye to recognize them.

Another matter that you might want to consider is that serious damage to an instrument does lower its value. You should be sure that your insurance covers not just the cost of the repair, but also recompenses you for the instrument's devaluation. A soundpost crack in a cello back might cost a few thousand dollars to repair properly, but if the instrument was worth several hundred thousand, the loss to you in devaluation is considerable. This is even more true for bows, where any damage can significantly affect their value. If the head comes off the bow, it can be repaired with a spline; the resale value of the bow, however, will be only a fraction of what it was before. There are two reasons for this depreciation in an otherwise sound instrument or bow: certain repairs (such as a soundpost patch) require grafting new wood into areas critical to the sound of the instrument or the playability of the bow. These are also the areas under the most tension, and therefore there is no way to guarantee that the repair will hold. Once damaged, a violin or bow will never be "as good as new."

The repairer who gives you the estimate for the repairs can also give you a letter detailing the damage and the devaluation to the instrument. There are no schedules for depreciation, as accidents vary in their severity and the resulting degree to which the instrument is harmed.

GENERAL MAINTENANCE

Aside from keeping your instrument well protected from accidents and extremes of temperature and humidity, little else is required from you in the way of maintenance—except for keeping it clean. Unfortunately, most new owners (and some longtime ones) tend to go after this with a vengeance, and they end up doing more harm than good. High-quality violin varnish is delicate and quite vulnerable to damage from common solvents and cleaners. It takes a professional touch to clean a violin properly—it is difficult to know where the grime ends and the varnish begins. During the cleaning process the varnish can be softened and even become tacky. If done inexpertly, the result can be more rag left on the violin than dirt on the rag.

Commercial cleaners and polishes don't really do the job—if they did, they would be dangerous to use. They are actually detrimental to your violin, for they are a combination of wax and linseed oil that will, through repeated use, build up and harden. Eventually you will end up with a second varnish, one that obscures the original and is very difficult to remove.

The best approach is to stop the dirt from building up in the first place. This means no more than using a very soft cloth to wipe the rosin off the top after each playing. An old cotton undershirt or handkerchief does well—just be sure it is clean and dry. The soft buffing of the cloth will also give your instrument a subtle sheen that you would never get with polishes, which leave your fiddle looking like a new car in the showroom, or a Christmas tree ornament.

You should resist the impulse to clean the fingerboard yourself. The only effective cleaner is alcohol, and it will run off onto the top faster than you can believe. It is dispiriting in the extreme to watch the varnish on the top of your violin melt before your very eyes—and if you try to rub it off quickly, you will have a real disaster. If you must clean the fingerboard, be sure to lay the instrument flat, put a piece of cardboard under the fingerboard to protect the top, and use a small piece of cotton that is almost dry. If you have an old or expensive instrument, just don't do it—it's not worth the risk.

THE BOW

Taking care of your bow is much less complicated than taking care of your instrument, but no less crucial. The most important thing to avoid is over-tightening it. When you are done playing, loosen the hair completely, and then bring it back just a single turn of the button. This will keep the hair even but allow the bow to relax, which is particularly important when the weather is cold and dry; the hair can shrink enough overnight to pull the head off a bow that has not been loosened.

Your bow will need rehairing when you feel that it is no longer digging into the string, or when you have lost a number of the bow hairs, or when they just get dirty from use. When the bow is rehaired, be sure that not too much hair is put on—this will lessen its playability and might harm the head or the frog. Also be careful not to use too much rosin. It is what gives bow hair a good grip on the strings, but too much will clog the hair, accumulate on the strings, and cause the bow to skate rather than grip.

Every now and then a bow needs to be recambered. How much camber is put in, and how it is distributed, will greatly affect the way the bow plays. If the bow seems sluggish, it might need more camber; if it has developed a wobble, it could need to be straightened. The process is delicate: The bow maker heats the bow over an alcohol flame to make it more malleable, then bends it over the edge of the workbench. As it cools, the pernambuco will retain the new curve. It's easy to scorch the wood or even break the stick. It may look like a simple job, but it's one that requires great skill and experience.

Keep the bow's grip and winding in good shape—both are there to keep your fingers from wearing down the wood of the stick or the frog. Such wear can be repaired, but it will lessen the value of your bow. If it wears quickly, you can have leather or plastic put over the end of the stick to protect the wood and the maker's stamp. Finally, remember that rosin can accumulate on the bow, and perspiration can wear it away. It's a good habit to wipe down the bow with a soft cloth after each playing, just as you do your instrument.

With a minimum amount of care, you can ensure that your bow will last as long as your violin.

Bridges. To the left, a blank for a violin bridge and, below, the finished bridge. Next, the blank for a cello bridge. The two finished cello bridges are the French bridge and, at the far right, the Belgian.

THE BRIDGE

The bridge and soundpost are the heart and soul of the violin. Perhaps no other single part can affect the sound as much as these two; their cutting, fitting, and proper placement are critical, both for the sound and for the health of the instrument.

The bridge is cut from a blank of specially selected, air-dried maple. The feet are cut with a knife to fit the top perfectly; the crown is then cut to give the strings the proper clearance off the fingerboard. This curvature is very important, as is the exact spacing of the notches for the strings; they will both affect the ease with which you can cross the strings or play one without hitting another. The bridge is then planed to its proper thickness and the cut-outs enlarged with a knife; these steps will determine the type of sound your violin will produce.

Cellists have a choice in the type of bridge they can use. By far the most common is the French model; the other is the Belgian, which has distinctively long legs and a small crown. It has less wood in it than the French; as you might suspect, it is used to open up the sound—to try for more volume or edge. However, it usually achieves this by sacrificing some of the richness of the sound.

A well-cut bridge can last for years and years, because it won't play out. You can enhance the life expectancy of your bridge by keeping it from warping (see next page). This is caused by the constant tuning of the strings, which gradually pulls the top of the bridge forward and stretches the wood out of shape. Make sure when you tune that the bridge has not been pulled forward; if it has, brace the body of the instrument with yours and, holding the top of the bridge firmly in both hands, gently pull it back toward you (page 34). It should move fairly easily; if it doesn't, loosen the strings slightly, then pull the top of the bridge back a little further than necessary, so that when you tune it back up to pitch, it will bring the bridge forward to the proper place. A little graphite from a soft pencil put under the strings in the grooves will help. Be sure to place a washcloth or small towel between the tailpiece and the top so that, if the bridge does fall over, the underside of the tuners won't gouge the top. You should be especially careful when you are replacing strings, particularly if you are

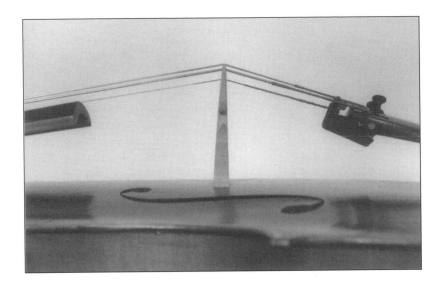

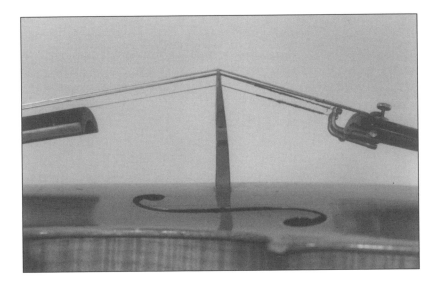

A straight bridge (above) and a warped bridge (below). Notice that the back of the straight bridge is not perpendicular to the level of the top; it should lean slightly forward. The warped bridge was not pulled back after changing strings or tuning, and it gradually bent. It can be straightened, although it will never be as strong.

putting on a new set, for this is when the bridge can be pulled far out of position. A warped bridge can be straightened, but, like a sprained ankle, it will never be as strong as it was.

Another part to keep an eye on is the parchment glued to the bridge over the grooves for the upper strings. These strings are quite thin and under a lot of tension; without this parchment for protection, they can quickly saw through the maple of the bridge. Check them as you change strings—if they appear to be worn through, get them replaced at once.

Most cellists find it necessary to have two or three bridges to compensate for the movement of the neck between the seasons. In the winter, the top dries out and the neck and fingerboard come up, making the strings feel low. On some instruments—particularly those with high arches—this difference can be significant. You can change the bridges yourself, if you have a tool called a bridge jack (page 35); but if you don't feel comfortable with it, your violin maker should be happy to do it for you. He or she can show you where the bridge should sit between the f-holes for the proper sound and response.

You can easily change the bridge yourself, as long as you exercise a minimum of caution. The primary concern is to keep the soundpost from moving or falling down (it is, after all, only wedged inside). Put the instrument on a folded towel on a table; to keep a cello from moving about, you might have to put a rolled towel under each end. Then loosen the strings slightly—not too much, since you don't want to pull the new bridge forward when you retune it. Place the bridge jack behind the bridge, and make sure it is straight before you tighten it (if it is leaning forward, it might fall over from the pressure). When you slip the old bridge out and the new one in, keep the feet in place, and just move the top; this will lessen the chance that the edges of the feet will scratch the varnish. Before you tighten the strings and take out the jack, make sure the bridge is standing straight and is positioned where your repairer showed you. Don't try to move it around after it is on—you might damage the top.

Pulling the bridge back. The important thing to remember is not to exert any pressure on the top as you rest your arms on it, for you might crack it. Direct pressure into your hands, to support the bridge, and pull the top back with only your forefingers. Placing your thumbs on the back of the bridge will keep it from going over backwards. If it won't budge, loosen the strings slightly and pull the bridge back a little farther than necessary.

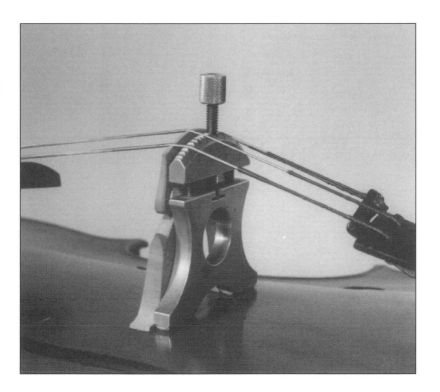

The bridge jack. Place it behind, not in front of, the bridge. Loosen the strings slightly before raising the jack to remove the bridge.

Setting the post (above). The soundpost is on the setter, ready to be placed in the violin. Fitting the post (below). This is a delicate job; an inexperienced hand can break the wing of the f-hole, in addition to gouging the inside of the top and back.

THE SOUNDPOST

The soundpost is the simplest piece to be found in your instrument, but by far the most difficult to fit and adjust. It is planed from a stick of well-seasoned, straight-grained spruce, and finished so that it is perfectly round and measures to an exact thickness. Even more important than the correct size is the fit when it is positioned in between the top and back of your instrument. If it is too loose or too tight, it will deform or even crack the top and will not give you the best sound. If it does not fit perfectly to the inside of the plates, it can tear them when it is moved during adjustment. A well-fitted post will be snug enough to remain standing when the strings are off, but not so tight that it takes a lot of force to move it.

Adjusting the post is best left to a person who has had training and experience. It looks easy, but if it is not done properly it can result in damage that you can't even see. A post is cut to stand perfectly straight inside the violin, and if it is not kept that way—even as it is being moved about—the edges of it can cut up the inside of the top or back. It also takes a long time to learn when the post can be moved, or when it has been taken as far as it can go without damaging the inside.

No instrument will stay in adjustment all the time. Violins, like people, are subject to the daily influences of weather and other vagaries; any position for the post is only the best for it most of the time. As the weather changes, so will the instrument; and even the most valuable violin will have a time of year when it is not happy. You should learn to differentiate between a temporary indisposition and a genuine slip in the adjustment.

It is easy to fall prey to the adjusting disease, embarking on a hopeless search for the perfect balance of sound and response. You will soon be trying for an idealized vision of what your instrument can do. Adjusting a soundpost is like tasting wine; after a short while you can lose your perspective.

A new instrument will need several longer soundposts as it plays in and the back stretches out. This is only to be expected. It can take up to a year before these changes start to stabilize. Remember, the wood has never been flexed before, and it is fairly elastic. If you have a new violin and it seems to have lost its sparkle or some of its punch, it probably just needs a new post.

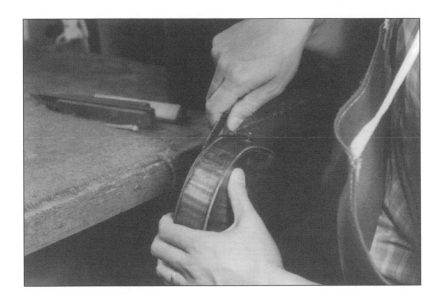

Fixing open bouts (above) looks like a simple job, but it's not. The joint mustn't be damaged during the repair, and the use of too much glue only causes further problems. Specialized clamps (below) are used to hold the bouts securely.

OPEN BOUTS

When the top or back come unglued from the sides, you have an open bout. The opening can be as small as a few millimeters, or as long as the full length of one of the curves. The important thing to remember is that, while irritating, it is easily fixed. In fact, an open bout can save your instrument from more serious damage, and you from a much more expensive repair. This is because the back and the top swell and shrink with changes in humidity; if this movement is drastic, a crack can develop—dryness is by far the most common cause of cracks. By coming free from the sides, the plates can move without cracking; thinner glue, which doesn't hold as firmly, is intentionally used to glue the top and back on for that very reason. In addition, light glue will help prevent damage to the edges if the top or back ever have to be removed for extensive repairs. A maker or repairer with any training at all will only use hot hide glue for this, because, being water-soluble, it is easily removable. And an experienced maker will try to use old, thin glue, since it will pop free quite easily.

Gluing bouts, like moving the soundpost, looks a lot easier then it is; trying it on your own can get you into a lot of trouble, some of which you won't even realize. The most common error is using the wrong glue, usually one that can't be taken off. Along with this is a tendency to overdo it—just a touch is enough to hold, but most amateurs will dump enough into the opening to glue a whole top on. Another problem is clamping; very few musicians have the proper clamps for this job, or have them set up correctly, or have the experience to know just how much they can be tightened without damaging the instrument. The most danger, though, comes from the glue knife itself. The gluing surface that holds the top or back to the rib structure is quite small, and if it is worn or damaged—or not properly cleaned—the glue will not hold. If the glue knife is not made or used just right, that surface can be irretrievably hurt, and the only way to fix it is to remove the top and back and rebuild the surfaces. All in all, gluing an open bout, while a small job, is one best left to a professional.

A worn upper bout. This is a common occurrence, and it can be easily retouched with new varnish. For those people who wear through varnish quickly, a thin piece of special transparent plastic can be applied here. It can also be put over the edge at the top of the c-bout, where the bow has worn through to the spruce.

RETOUCHING

Certain areas of the varnish on your instrument will wear down as you play, and it will inevitably pick up nicks and scratches. Some varnishes wear much faster than others or show the effects of bumps and scrapes more. Some musicians perspire quite freely while playing, and they can wear through the varnish swiftly (perspiration contains a lot of salt, which can act as a corrosive on the varnish, the wood itself, and even the strings). The area that tends to wear fastest is at the upper right rib and edges (see photo at left), where you shift into higher positions and where it is natural to hold a violin when you aren't playing it. Another area on a violin that wears quickly is the lower left rib and back, where it is held against your neck while you play. New varnish is frequently applied to all these places, and to any others where the wood has been laid bare; this is done even on the most valuable instruments. However, the proper varnish must be used—one that is easily removable—and the wood underneath has to be thoroughly cleaned of all dirt and oil and then smoothed, or the new varnish will not adhere. It is, of course, better to attend to this before you get to the bare wood, as it is a lot easier to replace lost varnish than wood. If you do wear through the new varnish on the shoulder and edges quickly, you might consider having a very thin piece of plastic tape put over the varnish to protect it. Your repairperson will use a special tape that will protect the varnish but is easily removed if necessary. It is frequently put on the ribs, particularly on valuable instruments where it is important to preserve as much of the original wood and varnish as possible, and it can even be put over the parts of the edge that are most susceptible to wear. The plastic is hardly noticeable, if done correctly, and has no effect on the sound. It is easily removed without any damage to the varnish or wood underneath.

As for nicks and scratches, they happen all the time, and you can console yourself with the thought that they always look a lot worse than they are. They can be filled and retouched so that they are, at worst, hardly visible. The important thing to remember is to keep the area clean. Do *not* put tape over it to protect it; this can be a disaster, as the adhesive on the tape will

The patina of age. The effects of use add to the character and beauty of the instrument, as this violin by Pietro Guarneri of Mantua, made in 1719, clearly shows.

get into the bare wood and also might be hard to get free from the varnish. While retouching varnish is durable, fine violin varnishes aren't and could easily be pulled off with the tape.

Another area that tends to show wear is the outer edge, particularly on cellos, as musicians tend to leave them resting on their sides. Again, it is an area frequently retouched, and some color and varnish will take care of the problem.

These scrapes and scratches are most noticeable on new instruments, where they really stand out. They can be retouched, but it is best just to relax and let them accumulate; after all, it is the wear that contributes to the beauty and allure of older violins (see photo at left). Like lines in a face, they add character, and they are an inevitable part of aging. Retouching on old instruments gets to be a problem when too much of it is done. This is a state of affairs that is becoming all too common; current taste calls for an evened-out look that requires extensive over-varnishing and polishing, in the process destroying the texture and patina of great old varnish. The result is a glassy, monochromatic finish that robs the instrument of its warmth and individuality. If you are lucky enough to have a fine old instrument, do not let an overzealous repairer sell you on the idea that it must be without imperfections and have a high shine. Once it has reached that stage, it can never go back, and you will have sacrificed one of the most valuable aspects of your instrument.

THE FINGERBOARD

The fingerboard is a part of the violin that also requires regular attention. It is made of ebony, which is a very hard and dense wood, but it will wear down with use. The fingerboard is shaped so that there is a slight dip (called the "scoop") planed in it lengthwise—from the nut to the lower end. This is done to provide additional clearance for the strings and help prevent buzzing.

The fingerboard will gradually develop grooves worn by the strings and hollows where your fingers rest; these have to be planed out, after which the board is scraped and polished to a mirror smoothness. The length of time between planings can be anywhere from one year to several, depending on the density of the wood, the amount you play, and the abrasiveness of your perspiration. Good ebony is becoming very difficult to find, so it is a good idea to go as long as you can between planings. At some point the fingerboard will be too thin to plane anymore and will have to be replaced, but if the instrument you have purchased has a healthy one of good, dense wood, this should not be necessary for many years. You might also keep in mind that making a proper fingerboard, and with it the neck, is one of the most difficult parts of setting up an instrument, and the one most often done poorly. The shape of the neck and fingerboard can have quite an effect on your perception of the instrument's response and ease of play. Many times the problems one encounters with the sound are actually due to the setup.

PEGS

Pegs that are well-fitted and maintained are a joy; those that aren't are a nightmare. The irony is that fitting them properly is not that difficult. As with the rest of the working parts of the setup, make sure that the pegs are fitted before you put down your cash. If done properly they should hold easily, without your having to press them into the pegbox, and turn smoothly, without binding or squeaking.

The pegs are originally cut with a tapered shaper that matches exactly the taper of the reamer used to cut the holes in the pegbox. If the tapers do not match exactly, the pegs won't hold. After fitting, the pegs are lubricated with peg dope, a commercially available product that, paradoxically, helps the pegs to both hold and turn freely. If the pegs squeak, they may just need more dope. If the noise persists, it may mean that the pegs are binding on one side and need fitting. You should try to avoid using the peg dope with too much abandon as it does build up and harden, at which point it all has to be cleaned out and the pegs refitted.

The weather can cause your pegs to bind or slip. Excessive humidity will make them swell; they can also bind in the fall as they dry out, and they'll need a sparing application of lubricant. You should never have to force your pegs to hold, or resort to such remedies as chalk. If things have come to this, the red light should go on; have some remedial work done. You run the risk of cracking the pegbox by leaving ill-fitting pegs unattended. This can be a very serious problem, as these cracks are hard to repair and can reopen, due to the stress placed on them. Properly repairing them requires gluing the crack, bushing (filling) the hole with wood, and finally refitting the peg.

Peg holes have to be bushed and recut when they are too worn and big for the pegs to fit them any longer. The holes can get just so large; beyond that point the shaft of the peg has to be made so large that it exerts too much pressure on the walls of the pegbox. In addition, it becomes very difficult to fine-tune the instrument with the pegs alone.

Pegs are usually made of ebony, rosewood, or boxwood. Unfortunately, the boxwood currently available bears little

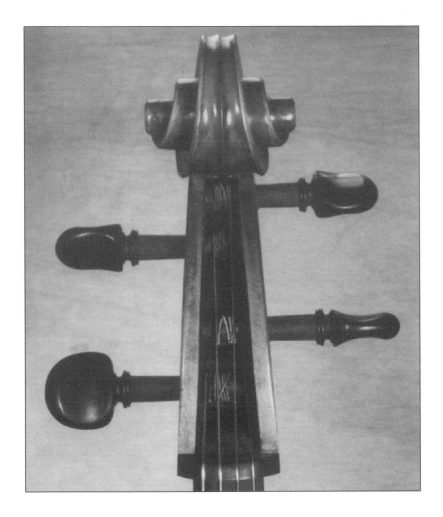

Winding the strings. First, in the hole, with just a bit extending; then one or two turns away from the pegbox; finally, cross back over and wind toward the pegbox.

resemblance to that found in the fine old English or Hill-style fittings. It is much softer and will compress easily as the peg is used, with the result that you will be faced with frequent refitting or replacement. A replacement wood, mountain mahogany, is now available in some fittings; it is every bit as tough, dense, and durable as boxwood used to be.

Be sure when you wind the strings around the peg that you do not let them bunch up against the pegbox wall. Some people are taught to do this as a trick to help the pegs hold; it is actually an easy way to cause a crack in the pegbox. With its taper, the peg is like a wedge, and winding the string in this manner just forces it deeper into the hole, eventually forcing the wood to give way.

You might find with a new instrument that the pegs need more frequent lubrication, and that they seem to wear into the holes much faster. This is because the wood of the pegbox is fresh and will absorb more of the dope and also compress more. This is natural, and it will soon cease.

BUZZES

Buzzes are the bane of the musician's (and the repairer's) life. They might be caused by something as simple as a loose E tuner, or as serious as an unglued patch on the inside. The frustrating part of it is isolating the culprit: any one of the myriad parts of the instrument—to say nothing of its repairs—could be the cause. Complicating matters is the fact that often a buzz will appear only under certain conditions—and almost never when you take it into the repair shop to be looked at. Many times there can be more than one buzz going on; the trick is to identify the bad one and then find its cause. The only way to do this is to eliminate the suspects one by one, and this can be a time-consuming and therefore costly job.

Buzzes almost always sound as though they are coming from the left f-hole, which is why people commonly blame them on a loose bass bar, which is virtually never the cause. When you begin the search—and you should look as much as you can before you head for the shop—check the strings first, since they will begin to buzz as they and their windings loosen. Next, check for open bouts, and then for anything loose in the setup, something on the tailpiece or chin rest, or even (not uncommonly) on the pegs. If you haven't found the cause by this time you will probably have to have it looked at by a professional. The most frequent cause of a buzz is purfling that has come unglued and is rattling in its channel, particularly on the top around the c-bouts. This can be the result of poor clamping at some point when an open bout was being glued and the edge was pulled away, opening up that channel. This can be taken care of, but the chances are very good that it will recur at some point. Any cracks will have to be checked to see if they are open or if their reinforcements inside have come loose, especially if they are near the bass bar. The box of the instrument functions solely as an amplifier for the vibrations produced by the bowing of the strings, so you should keep in mind that a pretty loud buzz can be caused by a very minor opening. No one can truthfully promise you that a buzz has been cured and banished forever; however slight, there is always the chance that it will return, no matter how much time, effort, and money have gone into tracking it down.

The decision to continue the search inside the instrument is one taken only as a last resort, as it will involve considerable time and expense. Once the top is off, anything that is loose on the inside could be the cause of the problem, and all the old repairs will have to be checked minutely and possibly redone. The problem is that none can be checked until the top is glued back on, so everything will have to be put right, and even then it might turn out to have been something not readily visible, and therefore overlooked.

The only consolation with a buzz—and it is mighty cold comfort—is that it takes one of truly heroic dimensions to carry more than a short distance. Incidentally, many shops will refuse to work on an instrument's buzz if it was purchased elsewhere, and they will refer you back to that shop for relief. This is not due to pique, but to their feeling—quite rightly—that the problem is directly related to the condition in which it was sold to you, and thus is the responsibility (and headache) of the person you got it from.

STRINGS

The choice of which strings to use on your instrument will have as much influence on the type of sound you will produce as any other single factor. You essentially have three kinds to choose from: gut, nylon, or metal.

Originally, violins were strung with plain, unwound gut strings, the lower ones sometimes braided for additional tension. (Although called cat gut by many, the material actually comes from the intestines of sheep.) At the end of the 17th century, however, plain gut strings could no longer meet the growing demands of musicians for increased projection and volume. Gut with various kinds of metal windings was tried, and, finally, just metal. In the past 30 years, various types of nylon have also been developed to substitute for gut. The windings for all these strings are usually made of aluminum, but you can also find silver, an alloy of silver and gold, chrome, nickel, tungsten, and even titanium. Interestingly enough, unwound gut strings have recently come back into use by some, with the resurgence of interest in Baroque performance technique.

When you select a string, you will also have a choice as to its gauge, which refers to how thick or thin it is. Keep in mind that the thicker the string, the more tension it will exert and therefore, one hopes, the stronger the sound. However, the desired result is not always produced, since the additional tension can also have the effect of choking the sound and just giving you a harder tone—more edge, but less quality. The thicker strings are called *forte;* the thinner, *dolce.*

Strings with a gut core tend to produce the richest sound. Their drawback is their susceptibility to variations in temperature and humidity, which can cause them to have an uncertain pitch. New types of nylon have solved this problem; these strings are more consistent and stretch out much faster. Their sound, though, tends to be brighter, with less core and more of an edge. They can cost significantly less than gut strings, a factor you might want to take into consideration.

Metal strings are essentially wire, wound or unwound, and they will give you the strongest, most edgy sound. They cut, rather than project, but on some instruments—usually those with a dark sound—they can sound the best. They do not vary in pitch, they last the longest, and they are the cheapest. Violinists invariably use an unwound metal E string, and most use Perlon and/or gut strings for the three lower strings. Violists will use a wound metal A, and cellists will add a wound metal D. Tungsten-wound C and G strings are popular with cellists in spite of their expense, because they offer the thinnest gauge without sacrificing any tension, and therefore they feel as though they have the fastest response. The wound gut lower strings are still used by some cellists, however, since it is hard to match the richness of their sound.

You can mix and match brands, types, gauges—whatever works to give you the best balance and tone to your instrument. The choice of strings is a very personal one; what works for you might not work for someone else playing the same instrument.

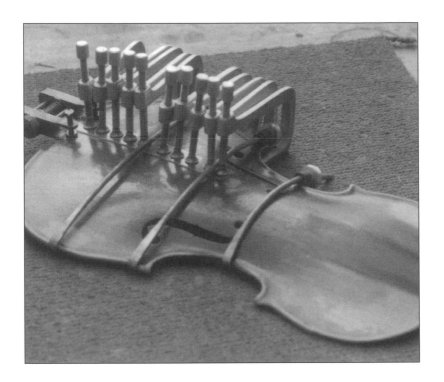

For a crack to be properly glued, the top has to be taken off.

REPAIRS

Even with the best care in the world, you might find yourself in need of a major repair or restoration at some point. Even for what might seem to be a straightforward job—a broken neck, for example—you will probably find that opinions about needed repairs, and estimates of their costs, vary substantially. This is due to the fact that nothing, when dealing with violins, is cut and dried; just as every instrument is unique, so will be the repair each one needs.

One of the concerns with any repair is how it will affect the sound; considering the sensitivity of most instruments, and the fact that virtually every part plays a role in the creation of its sound, it is a valid concern. It's a dilemma, but, unfortunately, an unavoidable one; the fact of the matter is that if the damaged area is not properly reinforced the instrument will not be playable, and a changed sound is better than none at all.

The most important factor in a successful repair is the first step: choosing the person to do it. Exercising discrimination now will save you from the very real possibility of greater expense and a continuing round of visits to other shops if the one you intially choose bungles the job. You would be surprised at how much of the work that comes through a shop consists of trying to save the patient not from the accident but from the doctor—undoing a bad repair. Unfortunately, redoing a bad job usually requires much more extensive work, while some repairs result in permanent damage.

You must remember that the field of violin making, repair, and restoration is completely unlicensed in the U.S.; anyone can get some stationery printed up and hang a sign out claiming to be a master restorer. The credentials and training of the repairer you choose to work on your instrument are much more important than the amount of the estimate; you find as often as not that better qualifications do not go hand in hand with higher prices. The violin field, for some reason, seems to have a high percentage of the self-taught, and you should avoid them at all costs, just as you would if you were looking for a doctor to operate on you. Find out where the repairer learned his or her skills. Try to find out his reputation among his peers, rather than among yours; an "ear for sound" or talent for

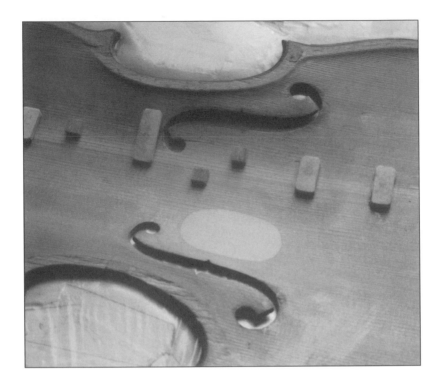

A soundpost patch is needed in this area of particular stress
and movement; it is inlaid to reinforce the repair of a crack.

adjusting does not guarantee skill in retouching. Most restorers of any repute cannot hide their distaste for inept colleagues, and it should not be hard to distinguish this from simple envy.

While the work is being done, don't rush the restorer. Wood can be capricious to deal with, and every job is different. Repairs, however, are alike in one regard: they always turn out to be much more time-consuming than expected. Owners always want the instrument back as soon as possible. That's understandable; many times it's the only one available, and you can't play the violin without the violin. Borrow one, if the repair shop doesn't have one to lend you, and then resign yourself to letting the repairer take the time necessary. This doesn't mean dropping out of sight; most repairmen have several jobs under way at any one time and can use some subtle prodding to keep yours on the front burner. Also, restorers invariably take a great deal of pride in their work and like to know that it is being appreciated. Don't hesitate to ask questions, but be prepared for some long answers.

While most of the work that goes on in a violin shop centers around routine maintenance, more serious repairs turn up regularly. The cause is not always an accident; the instrument or bow may be suffering from a repair done some time ago that has failed, or merely from the effects of heavy use. Although most older instruments look completely healthy from the outside, you would be surprised at how much repair work most of them have had. (Usually it takes a trained eye to see it—aside from the fact that a large part of the effort that goes into a repair is made to camouflage it, most of the work is hidden inside.) Virtually any instrument made before 1800, for example, has had the two most basic repairs, a neck graft and new bass bar. This is because, as musicians around the turn of the century began to require more projection and power from their instruments, they put more tension on these two vulnerable areas.

Repairs are done basically for three reasons—to fix damage; to add wood where there is not enough, causing the original material to be weak; or to improve the sound of an instrument. A brief explanation of what is involved in basic repairs might help you if you are ever in a position to have work done on your instrument.

Cracks are the most common form of damage. The top and back of your instrument are, comparatively speaking, quite thin: for a violin, standard thicknesses of the plates range from

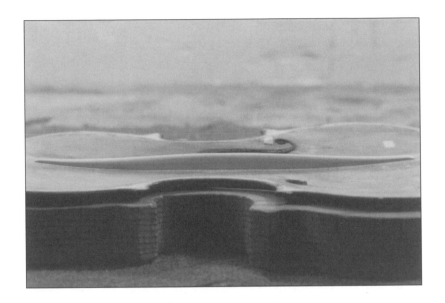

The bass bar's shape will affect the response and power of the instrument, as well as the openness of the sound. Shaping the bass bar, however, is an art, determined more by feel than numbers.

2.5 mm to 3 or 4.5 mm in the center. That's not much, considering the amount of force exerted on the instrument when it is strung up and played, but it allows for a delicate balance; the plates have to be strong enough to withstand indefinitely the tremendous pressure exerted on them without seriously deforming, but they have to be flexible enough to provide the mobility and resonance that creates the sound. Add to this the fact that when an arch is carved out of the wood it creates inequalities of strength, and that the weaker areas are just where the most strength is needed, and it is easy to see why cracks in older instruments are not uncommon.

When a crack does open up, the only proper way to repair it is to take the top off the instrument first (see photo on page 52), although unfortunately not all instruments are worth the expense and time of doing this. The reasons for having the top off are twofold: It is of paramount importance for the crack to be perfectly flush when it is glued, and the only way to achieve this is by using clamps down the entire length of the crack. The other reason is to reinforce the crack. The gluing surface of the crack itself is not enough to insure that it will not separate again, so small pieces of wood called studs are carefully fitted over the underside of the crack, where they act as permanent sutures. The fear of changing the instrument's sound when repairing cracks is real, but it is, of course, possible to minimize the effect. One method that is actually quite old but coming back into vogue involves the use of parchment as studs rather than wood. Parchment holds the wood together as effectively as wood, but it's more flexible.

Once the crack is properly glued and reinforced, it must be retouched so that the bare wood is properly sealed and the appearance of the damage is blended with the surrounding area. A common misconception among musicians is that a visible crack is a badly repaired one. Older cracks tend to show and can even turn black with age, since the glue that is used is hydroscopic—it absorbs moisture out of the air, and, with it, ambient dirt. The glue itself can also become discolored by the acid naturally found in wood. These dark cracks can still be holding fine; and even if they move a bit, it doesn't necessarily mean that they must be redone. Remember, the whole instrument is moving and vibrating while you're playing it.

A crack can also show if the natural patina of the old varnish has been preserved, for it will have the irregularities of a

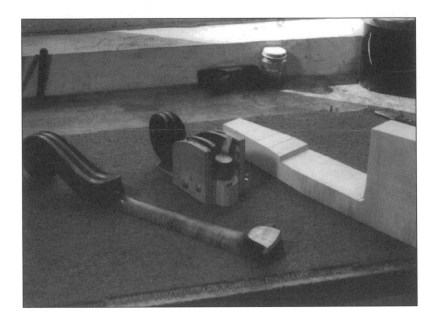

The neck at left has suffered a break in the most vulnerable area and needs a neck graft. At right is a scroll ready to be fitted with a new neck. When it is finished, a new finger-board will also be made and the new neck, with the original scroll, will be reset in the body of the instrument.

lifetime of wear; a newly retouched crack will be more even and shiny. Unfortunately, the mania for invisible cracks means that much unnecessary retouching is done. Since the narrow line of a retouching job cannot be made to match the old varnish, the original varnish is often overcoated and polished up to match the crack. You should be aware that the purity of the varnish of an antique instrument is a large part of its value, and that the larger world views such overvarnishing and polishing as vandalism. So if it becomes necessary to have a crack repaired on your instrument, be sure that the shop you intend to patronize does not have a reckless hand with the brush. How do you find out? Ask around. Restorers with any sense of self-respect have a hard time keeping to themselves their opinions of colleagues who are in the habit of debasing these irreplaceable antiques. Unnecessary restoration has become a plague, and owners would be well advised to consider quite seriously whether the work being recommended needs to be done. If the reason given is just that the damage is visible, that's not good enough. Old instruments are—well, old; cracks are to be as expected as the other signs of age and wear. Regluing them and retouching them doesn't make them go away, any more than pancake makeup makes wrinkles disappear.

There are some cracks that do need to be securely repaired, and two of these are soundpost and bass bar cracks. The reason that they must be solid is that they carry a good part of the stress exerted on an instrument. The bass bar supports one side of the top, distributing the pressure exerted by the bridge along its length. On the other side, the soundpost supports the top and transmits the vibrations to the back. Since the post is set a short distance behind the bridge, and not right under it, the downward pressure of the bridge is not directly opposed. This, added to the fact that the bridge area is the part of the instrument that moves the most when the strings are bowed, means that the thin wood of the top over the soundpost is subjected to the constant effects of both pressure and motion. Even the slightest crack in this area will very likely travel if it is not properly glued and reinforced. In this case, a simple stud won't hold the crack; a stud can help keep it together, but it can't secure it against this different sort of stress.

The proper repair is a patch (see photo on page 54). A patch is a new piece of wood inlaid into the old and then feathered to the original thickness; it is actually replacing old wood with new. The crack is glued, the surrounding area is carved out, and then a new piece of wood is carefully fitted in. Since the original wood is taken quite thin—sometimes only a few tenths of a millimeter before the patch is put in—a counterpart has to be made to support the area while it is being worked on and then while the patch is glued and clamped in place. Traditionally this counterpart was made of wood that was laboriously carved, planed, and then scraped to fit the top exactly. Now, however, most repairers make a cast, usually of plaster. If the wood being patched is deformed, the counterpart can itself be reshaped so that the reinforced plate regains its original shape.

A soundpost patch is not always done to reinforce a crack; sometimes it has to be done to replace the gouging and scarring that result from the cumulative effect of a badly fit soundpost. While both the top and the post are of spruce, there is a crucial difference: the direction of the grain. It is the hard endgrain of the post that rests against the much softer sides of the grain in the top, making it easy for the sharp edges of the post to damage the top. The soundpost is a simple length of spruce dowel; but its effect on the violin, tonally and structurally, is second to none. Learning to fit one properly is a matter of training, and you would be surprised at how few repairers can do it. Seek out someone who can.

It used to be that a soundpost crack in the top would devalue an instrument by ten percent. Nowadays, an old Italian instrument without a top crack is rare enough that a higher price is more of a premium than a norm. A soundpost crack in the back is an entirely different matter, however; that can devalue an instrument by up to 40 percent. This is because a soundpost crack in the back, even if properly repaired, is still problematic. The reasons why become clear when you think about it from the perspective of the forces exerted on the instrument. On the top, bass bar and soundpost cracks are under some opposing forces—the bridge pushes down, but the soundpost and bass bar push up. On the back, however, the post pushes out, with nothing to help resist the constant pressure. If you look at the back of an old fiddle, you will almost always see that the wood has deformed so that the high point of the arch is over the soundpost. So even when the crack is glued and patched, the pressure on it, which makes it want to open up again, is unopposed. There are also other reasons why it is less secure. As we just saw, the soundpost area is the high point of the back arch—so when the violin is put down, it is lying on the crack. In addition, maple doesn't hold glue as well as spruce, and it is much harder to retouch convincingly. Last of all, the back is much thicker than the top at the point where the post rests, so, if a patch is put in, more of the original wood has to be removed for the new wood to be feathered in. As with the top, you will occasionally find that a patch has been put into a back where there is no crack; in this case, it is to add thickness. A thin back takes the richness and kick out of the response, and many times a doubling is put in to give the instrument the extra focus and power it may be lacking. Such a patch is found frequently in older Italian cellos, particularly those with poplar or willow backs.

Technically, the process might be the same as repairing a cracked top, but a soundpost crack in the back is probably the most difficult job that a repair shop sees. If you are ever faced with one, seek out the most qualified person you can find; and, again, if it is an old crack that is visible but holding, don't let anyone convince you that it needs to be redone. Repairing violins is not climbing Mount Everest, and "just because it's there" is not a valid line of reasoning.

A bass bar crack requires the same thorough treatment as a soundpost patch, although the approach is somewhat different. To repair any damage properly, the repairer has to have a good grasp of the way the violin moves and vibrates; once the movement is understood, the method of repair follows naturally. In the case of the bass bar, it plays a dual and somewhat conflicting role—it both stiffens the top and aids in its vibration. In supporting the top, the bass bar plays the same role that the soundpost does under the other side of the bridge. The difference is that rather than transmit the vibrations to the back, the bass bar distributes them along the top. The top, without the bar, would flex much more—at least in the short time before it collapsed from the pressure. The bass bar is shaped to find the proper balance between freedom of movement and adequate support (see photo on page 56). When a crack develops, it usually runs on top or just along the side of the bar itself; this is because the top flexes over the bar like a hinge. The proper repair for a bass bar crack is to reinforce it with studs, which run under the bass bar. The only way this can be done without resorting to magic is to remove the old bar, glue the crack, fit the new bar, and then—before gluing in the new bar—fit and glue studs over the crack. Once they are shaped, the new bass bar is then refitted to account for the studs—a complicated job, but the only way to ensure that the crack will hold. Does it stiffen the top, and thus affect the sound? Yes—but the chances of an unreinforced crack holding are slim; and many times, on an old instrument, the additional strength over the bar is all to the better.

The neck of the violin is another part of your instrument that might someday need replacing, especially if it was worn when you purchased it. While the thickness of the neck is important—one that is too thin is more susceptible to warping and moving with the changes in the seasons—its shape is of equal concern. A properly shaped neck is one that lets you shift from string to string and through all the positions without feeling any bumps or edges; as you might imagine, carving one properly is one of the most demanding jobs of making or setting up an instrument. The way the neck is set is just as critical for the violin's sound. The angle of the neck, and its tilt, help determine the amount of pressure the strings exert on the top, and thus the way the body resonates. Neither resetting the neck nor taking the more drastic step of making a new one should be undertaken lightly; either one involves cutting the old neck out of the body, replacing wood, and changing the way your instrument feels, sounds, and responds (see photo on page 58).

With any repair, be sure that all the steps and their consequences have been fully explained to you, and don't proceed unless you are certain that the repairer who has proposed it has the training and expertise to undertake the operation. As with a surgeon, an eagerness to grab the knife should be a warning sign for you to go away and think it over, or get a second opinion. Of course, all costs should be fully laid out, in writing, before any work is undertaken; and if a revision is necessary, ask to see the work and have it fully explained.

You may never personally encounter the procedures described above. If you do, just remember that all these repairs, while serious, are commonly found in the workshop, and if properly done they will not interfere with your ability to use your instrument as freely or with the same satisfaction as before. Just be sure that you find someone qualified to do the work, and that he or she explains to your satisfaction not just what needs to be done but why it is necessary.

All you really have to do to keep your instrument and bow in good condition is to be careful. Violins are remarkably durable if treated well, and they respond to care. If you exercise a minimum amount of caution and prevention, you will never have to think about finding another. You can save all that energy for practicing and playing.

About the Author

James N. McKean is a violin maker and restorer in New York City, as well as a corresponding editor to *Strings* magazine. After graduating from the Violin Making School of America in 1977, he spent several years in the atelier of Vahakn Nigogosian, learning the fine points of restoration and setup, before opening his own shop in 1982. He is a member of the American Federation of Violin and Bow Makers and has won awards for violin making in several international competitions.